Motschi von Richthofen

Mia Bavarians verstengan d'Leut

Gedichte/Poems
English/German

tredition GmbH
1. Auflage 2015

Copyright 2015 by
Motschi von Richthofen und
tredition GmbH

tredition GmbH
Sitz der Gesellschaft: Hamburg
E-Mail: info@tredition.de
Geschäftsführung: Sönke Schulz, Sandra Latußeck

ISBN: 978-3-7323-3672-2 (Paperback)
ISBN: 978-3-7323-3673-9 (Hardcover)
ISBN: 978-3-7323-3674-6 (e-Book)

Simplicity is the most difficult thing to secure in this world; it is the last limit of experience and the last effort of genius.

George Sand

Die Natur ist die große Ruhe gegenüber unserer Beweglichkeit. Darum wird sie der Mensch immer mehr lieben, je feiner und beweglicher er werden wird. Sie gibt ihm die großen Züge, die weiten Perspektiven und zugleich das Bild einer bei aller unermüdlichen Entwicklung erhabenen Gelassenheit.

Christian Morgenstern

Deutsche Gedichte

Bayerische Ansichten

Der Bayer ist immer guad drauf
Auch wenn er zwida is
Denn am Ende is es ja wurscht
Wia der Herrgott des so mog
Und nicht zu vergessen
Der Deife hat ja auch mitzuredn
Sacklezement wias is so is
Und gfrei ma uns auf den nächsten Tag
Servus sagn ma der Sonn
Auf am Riedastoa
Mai hamm mirs schee

Entsnowden

Die Wahrheit zu entfesseln
hat einen bitteren Beigeschmack
denn man lässt die Katze aus dem Sack

Immer schon ein Fall
Ob Eva's oder Adams Sträflichkeit
An Menschenrechten fehlt es weit

Geächtet ist man gleich
Wie konnte man es nur wagen
Und die das Geheime sagen

Die unbegrenzten Möglichkeiten
scheinen nicht zu existieren
und an Vertrauen zu verlieren.

Aufzeichnungen von allem
Kontrolle über jeden Schritt
Was für ein kranker Ritt.

Promiskuität

Für was ne Beziehung
Es sind meine Menschenwürde
Und meine Entscheidung
Unser Verhalten ist autonom.

Offenherzig und freizügig
Im Vorfeld bereits abgesprochen.
Es ist wie ein Spring Break
Anhaltend ein Tag oder gar Wochen.

Unsere Genussehe auf Zeit
von einer halben Stunde bis 99 Jahre
Je nach innerer Gegebenheit
ist die Dauer recht unterschiedlich.

Verwerflich wohl kaum,
denn selbst in der Natur
hat jede Art ihren Raum,
um sich auszuleben.

Eventuelle Disparität der Erwartungen
von Partnern zueinander
muss schnellstens bereinigt werden
fürs harmonische Miteinander.

Jedem das Seine
Und mir das Meine

Abstellgleis

Ich heiße altes Eisen
gehöre zu den Greisen
die nur noch Brei speisen
und die Welt bereisen

Und nicht mehr produktiv
Geschweige denn positiv
zur Gesellschaft beitragen,
sondern nur noch klagen.

Weit gefehlt ich bin fit
halte mit den Jungen mit
agiere wie in eh und je
da ich das Ganze seh

Alter ist nicht wichtig
Für vieles nichtig
Man wird nachsichtig
Das ist richtig.

Dilettantismus

Prätentiös und rigoros
Ganz apathisch aber mit obszönen Worten
Beschreibt er emphatisch seine Apprehensionen

Subtil wäre es besser gewesen,
aber maliziös war es ihm lieber,
Bloß keine Blöße geben

Ungeniert konstatierte er die Dekadenz.
Degustation der Wortwahl auf niedrigem Niveau

Er war wohl neurasthenisch
und manchmal auch apathisch

Ein prekäre Situation wurde moduliert
und alles war nur ostentativ

Was für ein abstruser Pathos,
welch ein Exemplar der Spezies

Das Dilemma der Verfangenen
in ihrer Welt.

Kurvendiskussion

Es fing an
mit dem Anstieg
immer höher und höher,
das Leben war gut zu einem.
Aktionen verfolgten immer ihr Ziel
und erreichten es mit einer Leichtigkeit.
A gmade Wiesen wie man so schön sagt.
Kein Widerstand, alles flutschte wie es sollte
Das nenn ich mal Glück auf allen Ebenen im Sein!
Wie das Leben so ist gibt es ja andere Zeiten
da kommen dann die Steine des Weges,
und man darf sie von dannen tragen.
Egal das gehört ja auch zum Sein!
Auf und nieder immer wieder,
besingen wir das Leben.
Amüsantes Streben
Hört nicht auf.

Foodgasm

Eine wahre Gaumenfreude
Genuss in Ekstase

Ein Feuerwerk der Geschmäcker
Hm fein wie lecker

Manchmal müssen wir in den Untergrund
Um das kulinarische zu finden.

Speisen der ganz besonderen Art
und oft nicht alla Card.

Das Wasser läuft im Mund zusammen
vermengt sich mir der Vielfalt.

Sensationen finden statt
und man ist papp satt.

Fappieren

Selbst ist der Mann
der sich bestimmen kann.

Wichtig denn nicht nur die Liebe
befriedet die Triebe.

Strotzen, glühen und verlangen,
damit hat alles angefangen.

Das Limbische System macht mit
intellektuell auf Schritt und Tritt

Für die Jugend ganz normal
ist ja oft auch optimal.

Bevor wir explodieren
heißt es fappieren.

Staffellauf

Ich habe eine Staffelei und male,
male die Zukunft als eine Vision,
indem ich im Staffellauf mitwirke.
Ich übergebe als Nächster
und zeichne alle Dinge, die ich sehe
ich renne und renne
Runden um Runden.
Wieder übergebe ich den Stab
immer wieder.
Von mir zu mir,
von meinem Ich zu meinem Ich,
von Sekunden zu Stunden.

Die Jahre vergehen,
ich halte das Ei in der Hand,
Columbus auf seiner Santa Maria
Ich fliege als Staffelkapitän,
meine Staffelei unter dem Arm.
Ich übernehme den Pinsel
und übergebe die Vorstellung,
schnell und zeitlos.

Mammon

Der gefallene Engel und reich
verbannt aus dem Himmelsreich
Schnöde weil nicht übersetzt
und mit Habgier vernetzt.

Jedermann hat es gezeigt
wohin der Geiz sich neigt.
Und hinter der ganzen Fassade
lauert die Milde und Gnade.

Kurz gesagt
hinter was man jagt
muss jeder selbst wissen
und seine Flagge hissen.

Mia san mia

Mai mia ham halt a Tradition
Und di lem ma a
Mia hab unser eigne Mission
Und des is die Natur
Unsere Kia ham a guats Lem
Mia san wief
Und ren a ab und diam an Schmarrn
Und d'Beag men ma narrisch gern
Und aufschbuin dema a recht gern
Des is net ausgschamd awo
Des is gscheid Lem lem

Miteinander

Wir sind Jahre zusammen
durch dick und dünn gegangen
unsere Kinder gross gezogen
gewechselt Windeln und Hosen

Unsere Liebe immer in Flammen
Unsere Seelen immer wieder eingefangen
immer geschwommen auf den Lebenswogen
und immer den Weg geschmückt mit Rosen

Wundervoll dieses Geschick
Ein unendlicher Blick
ins Reich der Liebe und Zweisamkeit
vom der Gegenwart in die Ewigkeit

Danke danke dir
Im Jetzt und hier

Sonne

In deinem Angesicht leuchtet mein Anlitz
In deinen Strahlen bade ich mich
Und auch wenn ich schwitz
mag ich dich

Wundervoll ist dein Farbenspiel
Wundervoll ist dein Schattenspiel
Wundervoll ist dein Abendlicht
Wundervoll ist dein Morgenlicht

Schnell bist du sehr schnell
Warm bist du sehr warm
Belebend bist du belebend
Bereichernd bist du bereichernd

Sonne Sonne Sonne
Du meine Wonne

Ein kleines Schloß

Hätte ich ein kleines Anwesen
dann hätte ich eine Bibliothek zum Lesen
Hätte Kühe und Pferde
und eine ganze Schafsherde
Hätte einen Garten reich
an Ost und Gemüse und nen Teich
Hätte Menschen die mir helfen
und nen Wald mit Elfen
Hätte eine grosse Garage
für die Automontage
Hätte einen Pool zum Schimmen
um den Körper zu trimmen
Hätte hätte vieles mehr
Einen Bootssteg zum Mittelmehr
und vieles anderes wie die Malerei
stünde meinem Aktionismus frei
Frei sich zu entfalten
und zu walten und schalten,
so freue ich mich am Jetzt und hier
und öffne meine Träumertür

Ameise

Eine Ameise kreuzt meinen Weg.
Kennt sie meine Gedanken, die ich heg?
Ganz gleich ob sie es weiß,
sie ist es, die den Weg mir heißt.
Ich sehe sie und step beside
to honor trace and sight.
Again I obey the silent voice
of the universe and our own choice.
Es sind wir selbst die entscheiden
und jede Zerstörung vermeiden.
Erschaffen heißt unsere Vision
Leben achten in jeder Dimension.
Und jede noch so kleine Kreatur
hat seine eigene Lebensspur,
die wir achten und wertschätzen
und mit unserem Sein vernetzen.

Die Seele schreit

Die Seele schreit und ist benommen
Sie hat schreckliches vernommen
Nichts konnte sie dafür machen
nicht wieder Lebenselexier entfachen
Ihr waren die Hände gebunden
und verursachte tiefe Wunden
Der Körper muss nun leiden
und alle Eingeweiden
Vernunft und nachhaltiges Denken
mein Schicksal lenken.
Ganz nett und letztlich eine Illusion
in jeder menschlichen Situation
Selbstzerstörung als moderne Waffe
viel intellegenter als der Affe.
Wie dem Dasein verzeihen,
wenn Seele und Körper schreien.

Krieg

Was kriege ich vom Krieg
und was kriegst du
Was ist es mit dem Sieg
gibt es kein Tabu
Gut für die Waffenschmiede
und der Arbeitswelt
und danach kommt der Friede
und mit ihm das Geld.

In dem Wahnsinn ist das der Sinn!
Großartig und sehr intelligent.
Welch grandioser menschlicher Gewinn
durch den Primaten-Dirigent.

Man muss sagen 'gut', und Loblieder singen,
wie weit diese Entwicklung Mensch schon ist,
gegenseitiges zerstören und erzwingen
was will man da mit einem Altruist?

Na die Evolution wird es ja wohl mal zeigen,
ob aus den Fehlern gelernt werden kann
wohin wir steigen und unser neigen
in unserem genialen Existenzplan.

Was kriege ich nun von dir?
und was kriegst du von mir?

Tradition

Von einer zur nächsten Generation
überliefert durch Kommunikation
werden geistreiche Flammen weitergegeben
Altes zum Neuem hinübergeben.

Überlieferung der Gesamtheit der Fähigkeiten
Wissen und Kultur verbreiten
soziales Verständnis und weises Handeln
ein fundamentales Wandeln.

Informationen zum Zweck der Erhaltung
als bewusst und unbewusste Überlieferung
Tradition als wichtiges Ankerseil
und kultureller Bestandteil.

Eine Basis für den menschlichen Umgang
und alle ziehen am gleichen Strang.

Schildkröte

Weit zurück bis ins Karnium
Reicht deine Existenz
Du hoch interessantes Individuum
Danke für deine Präsenz

Du bist die Mutter der Schrift
Dein Panzer war das Fundament
Die 0 die auf die 1 trifft
Das Kommunikationsexperiment

Du siehst mit deinen Augen
Eine Farbenpracht so wunderbar
Ich kann es kaum glauben
4 Farbenklang für wahr

Viel besungen
Du altes Wesen
Viel errungen
Was wir lesen

Tierischer Panzer

In der Marine lang gewesen
Timothy du altes Wesen

Panzer rollen
Vernichten und töten
Ein Militärgrollen
Gepaart mit Nöten

Nicht dein Ansinnen
Ein anderes Gewinnen
Kommunikation geben
Gedanken verweben

Einen Schutz suchen
Ruhe verbuchen
Ewigkeit im Innern
Unendliches Erinnern

Aussen hart und innen weich
Eine Einzigartigkeit
Just unglaublich reich
Im Panzerkleid

Schloss Powderham nach Jahren
Nachdem du zur See gefahren

Klanggeflüster

Warum den Worten Musik einflösen
und die Zeit beschreiben
Warum die Buchstaben spielem lassen
und Zeitloses schreiben.
Wer kann es hören, die volle Poesie
und mit ihr schwingen
Wer erfühlt die Tiefe ihrer Klänge
und wird mit ihr singen.
Wie die Zeilen mit den Wellen verbinden
und das Gehör ausbilden
Wie die Gemüter öffnen für Neues
und das Empfinden bilden
Fragen über Fragen
was kann ich sagen
nichts nur das Eine
ne Antwort gibt es Keine

Reichmut und Armtum

Im Reichtum
the soul just bloom
In der Armut
felhlt der Mut
Der Reiche ist arm
Der Arme reich

Die Hand

Die Hand
ist recht gewandt.
Sie formt und erschafft
Sie transformiert Gedankenkraft

Die Hand
wird oft verkannt.
Sie greift und versteht
Sie ist's die neue Wege geht

Die Hand
ist auch verwandt
mit allen genialen Kreationen
und oft Macher von Visionen.

Die Kümstlerhand
kreiert allerhand
Blickt über den Tellerrand
gleich Kant

Es ist allerhand
mit dieser Hand.
Sie verändert auf die Schnelle
als handwerklicher Geselle.

Es ist altbekannt,
das die Hand,
unser Sein in den Händen trägt
und unsere Zivilisationsgeschichte prägt

Ohne dich wär die Menschheit
sicherlich nicht so weit
Du Prunkstück der Natur
Du Erschaffer von Kultur.

Dank dir Hand
Als Verwandler vom Verstand

Dank dir Hand
Unser wunderbarer Goldbestand

Könner

Könner brauchen Gönner,
denn Neider sind ja viel gescheiter
und gewähren dir keinen Ruhm.

Drum suche die Unterstützer,
denn sie sind die Beschützer
deines Könnens und dir's gönnen.

Die Neidhammel haben nur Bammel
und besitzen weder Stil noch Profil.

Grosses wird von Grossem protegiert
und das ganz frei und ungeniert.

Zigaretten

Manchmal gelüstet es mir sehr
Dieser Genuss und das Inhalieren
Und es fällt mir äusserst schwer
Nicht meine Sucht zu stimulieren

Ach Busch ich war ja so krank
Jetzt rauch ich wieder, Gott sein Dank!
Gerne würd ich's mit dir halten
und meine Begierde entfalten

Wie's halt nun mal ist
Adieu und auf ein andermal
Jeder hat seine Lebensfrist
und die Qual der Wahl

Gewohnheiten sind Vergangenheit
und keine Zigarette weit und breit.
Die Versuchung war ohne Gelingen
und konnten den Schweinehund bezwingen.

Anmut

So voller Grazie und Mut
erleuchtest du den Weg
du bist mir der Tropfen Wermut
und für Schönheit der Beleg.

Ohne Zwang und gänzlich frei
trägst du würdevoll den Tag in dir
gleich sinnlich/geistiger Malerei
die Harmonie als Lebenselexier

Die schöne Seele zeigt ihr Kleid
grazil und voller Würde
sie erhellt durch ihre Heiterkeit
und überwindet jede Hürde.

Bayerischer Humor

Wenn a Bayer di mog
dann schießt er dich hinauf
Scherzerl auf deine Kosten
denn es soll ja nicht rosten
der heitere Kreislauf
im Lebenssog.

Über sich selbst gar
lacht der Bayer am Besten
dann kann er auf den Wolken singen
und das Hosianna anklingen,
denn am Beliebtesten
ist der Schmunzelaltar.

Und wenn's der Herrgott will
is der Bayer ganz still
und denkt sich „ja Mai"
is ja ganz einerlei
Griesgram ist nicht angesagt
und wird glai wie der Teufel verjagt.

Reichtum ist das Wichtigste

Welch grosser Reichtum
daran mag jeder gerne naschen.
Mit stetem Wachstum
füllen sich deine Taschen

Welch herrlicher Palast!
Hier ist man gern zu Gast
und erfreut sich an der Pracht,
die das Sein fantastisch macht

Welch fantastische Persönlichkeit
mit aufrichtiger Herzlichkeit
Deine innere Wärme gibt Kraft
Eine genial Eigenschaft

Welch großartiger Wohlstand
Just durch dein Wesen.
Dein immaterieller Geldbestand
ist Handverlesen

Üppig und voller Phantasie
sprudelst du vor Energie
Dein fruchtbarer Boden
hat mich empor gehoben.

Du bist reich das ist wichtig
und all das Andere nichtig.
An deinen Gaben
kann man sich laben.

Das sind sie die Werte
nicht mit Gold zu erkaufen.
Als grandioser Seelenexperte
Bereicherst du die Menschenhaufen

…

Reichtum ist das Wichtigste

Leichtigkeit

Alles ist so schwer
ich kann nicht mehr
will mal nur lachen
und Unsinn machen
Jede Sekunde nützen
getarnt mit Narrenmützen
Auf zur Leichtigkeit
denn was letztlich bleibt
ist ein gutter Scherz
und das Lächeln im Herz

Der Teppichhändler

Eines der ältesten Handelsgüter
Fein gewebt von Menschenhand
Erfreut die modebewussten Gemüter
ganz gleich ob auf dem Boden oder an der Wand.

Den Räumen Schönheit zu verleihen
danach steht ihm Sinn und Leidenschaft
So reist er in ferne Ländereien
auf abenteuerlicher Wanderschaft.

Weit über den Orient hinaus
führt ihn die Freude an den Stoffen
Immer wieder für neue Muster offen
aus dem Bauchgefühl und frei heraus.

Er ist ein Zauberer der großen Flächen
und gibt ihnen ein neues Gesicht
Er entwickelt aus kreativen Gesprächen
ein harmonisches Gleichgewicht.

Seine Kunden entführt er in eine Welt
nach tausend und eine Nacht
In den Palast oder ins Beduinenzelt
und erzählt von der reichen Pracht.

So betreibt er das Gewerbe
und macht dabei Gewinn
voller Stolz und Frohsinn
es ist sein wunderbares Erbe.

The carpet dealer and his art
Timeless beauty as a part.

Das Gewicht der Zeit

Zeit ist relativ so Einstein
Und es stimmt zum Teil
Und auch ein endloses Seil
In unserem wichtigen Sein

Haben wir das Glück
So überleben wir unsere Kinder
Und geben ein Stück
Zurück an die Enkelkinder

Und wenn wir dann gehen müssen
Ist das Loslassen unglaublich schwer
Und wir werden uns vermissen
ein Part von uns wird ganz leer

Jede Sekunde war eine Wohltat
Und sie wächst in unserer Seele weiter
So ist es mit dem Lebensrad
Man ist Vater Mutter oder Wegbegleiter

Und so hat Gewicht
Man glaubt es nicht
Die Zeit der Emotionen
Frei von zeitlichen Impressionen.

Generationen

Sind es die Grenzen der Menschheit,
die sich dauernd anreihen
an jene der raumlosen Ewigkeit
und uns Toleranz verleihen.

Unsere Seelen sind es die begreifen
und neue Wege begehen,
allen Widrigkeiten entgegenstehen
und nach den Sternen greifen.

Der wahre Humanismus wird siegen
und die Lächerlichkeit bekriegen
denn das Gute ist voller Kraft
indem es kreiert und schafft.

Im Universum werden wir lesen
mit dem ehrenwert und gütigem Wesen,
wie ein Virus, die Welt heimsuchen
und Siege verbuchen.

Neue Generationen werden kommen
und als aufweckender Spiegel fungieren
denn die Zukunft wird ersonnen
um Weitsicht und Liebe zu formieren

So verändern die Generationen
und geben der Zeit ein neues Bild
sie haben ihre eigenen Visionen
und gegen Idiotien ihr Schild.

Alles ist möglich, alles hat seine Zeit
so auch für die Menschheit.

Verhaltensgestört

Es gibt Exemplare
bei denen fehlen so einige Tassen
die hat der Vogel wohl mitgenommen
und wo anders stehen gelassen.

An dessen Stelle
hat er sich im Kopf wohl breitgemacht
und zwitschert sein eindimensionales Lied
von der enormen Geistespracht.

Während er so singt
lösen sich auch noch die Schrauben
und man hört wie es kracht und knackt
und ihn um seinen Verstand berauben.

Das Synapsen-Konzert
mit Tönen, die nur noch so springen
ein Auf ein Ab oder ein Hin ein Her
und mit dem Wahnsinn ringen.

Und sehr amüsant
oft wird es nicht erkannt.
Und sie laufen weiter herum
denn sie sind ja nicht dumm.

Hausse und Baisse

Auf und ab
nur nicht zu knapp
Wie das Leben
am Anfang die Reben
dann die Frucht
eine exquisite Zucht
und man greife
mit der Reife
den gewinnreichen Ertrag
ein akzeptabler Betrag

Und auf die Schnelle
wie auf der Welle
bricht sie wieder ein
und der bittere Wein
ergründet die Tiefen
unter ferner Liefen
Die Kurve geht nach unten
hat den Peak überwunden
und strebt wieder nach oben
um den Hausse zu loben

Gladiatoren und Genies

Dante mit dem göttlichen Talent
Wird umschwärmt und hochgehoben
Gell-Mann weltbewegend-exzellent
Erhält die noblen Roben

Den einen kennen unendlich viele
Denn es sind die Muskelspiele
Die begeistern und inspirieren
Und die alle Völker adorieren

Die anderen kaum bekannt
Scheinen wohl interessant
Nur sind sie zu weit weg
Und haben keinen Vermarktungszweck.

Beide verbinden auf ihres Weise
Emotionen und Grenzen
Beide ziehen ihre Kreise
Visionen und Sequenzen

Du

du bist wundervoll
in dem was du versuchst zu bewegen
du bist wundervoll
durch dich kann sich vieles Neue regen
du bist wundervoll
und für viele ein menschlicher Segen
du bist wundervoll
und konntest vieles hinweg fegen
du bist wundervoll
und hast deine ganz eigenen Stärken
du bist wundervoll
wir lernen alle jeden Tag zu bestärken

sicher wir sind nicht perfekt
und haben alle einen Defekt
dennoch will unsere Seele geben
und Sinnvolles gestalten im Leben

du und ich wir alle versuchen
zu backen einen speziellen Kuchen
mit den Zutaten unserer Vorstellungen
als menschliche Bereicherungen.

du bist und ich bin
wir alle haben einen Sinn.

Burnout

Schneller ist die Zeit
in unserer Geschäftigkeit.

Was gerade erfunden
ist schon wieder verschwunden.

Mobilität ganz hoch geschrieben
hat die Ruhe vertrieben.

Wir scannen nur noch schnell,
als neuzeitige Wilhelm Tell.

Gerade in den Grossstädten
liegen wir in Zeitketten.

Fliegen um die ganze Welt
mit uns das Wachstumszelt.

Ausgebrannt und verkohlt
haben wir uns eingeholt.

Prima das nenn ich klasse
grossartig diese Menschenrasse.

Wikileaks

Da hat einer mal die Wahrheit gesprochen
und wäre fast ersoffen
Blubb blubb
Den ertränken wir mal flink
Die Wahrheit verträgt nicht jeder.
Aufdecken kann man ja dies und das
Nur das was wichtig ist bleibt verborgen

Pressefreiheit gibt es auf dem Papier
nicht aber im Netz
Die Wahrheit gefangen im Netz
Spinnst du denn?

Die Fuchsjagd kann beginnen.
Wir gewinnen.

Heurika
Jetzt ist es klar

Weltklimagipfel

Das ist ja wohl der Gipfel
Ihr da mit dem Politzipfel

Super seid ihr für eure Kinder unterwegs
Diskutiert palavert und depattiert

100 Punkte für die Meister
sie werden immer dreister

Worin sind sie nur gefangen?
Worin haben sie sich denn verfangen?

Hoffe ihr habt gut gegessen
und dabei das Wichtigste vergessen.

Aufruf zur Weitsicht
Aufruf zu Taten
Aufruf zur Nachhaltigkeit
Aufruf zum Verändern

Wir setzen uns ein für die Rechte
unserer Natur und all ihren Lebewesen.

Wachstumsbeschleunigungsgesetz

Wir beschleunigen das Wachstum

Nach einem Tief kommt ein Hoch

Mehr und schneller, das unterstützen wir
und machen Gesetze

Weniger Steuern und mehr Geld
Der Fisher vorm Herrn

Ist eine einfache Formel
Und das beherzigen wir

Wachstum wachstum über alles
Wachstum für das Vaterland

Heurika ja Heurika
der Wachstum ist da

Multipolare Welt

Die Abhängigkeit, die zwischen Staaten existiert,
bestimmt unsere Gesellschaft.
Die Verwundbarkeit eines Staates
Ist abhängig von der Verteilung der Machtmittel

Im 15. Jahrhundert begann der Aufstieg des Westens,
im 19. Jahrhundert der von Amerika
jetzt China, Indien und Süd Amerika
und in der Zukunft Afrika

Multipolarität ist kein Wert
Sie ist Fakt in unserer Zeitgeschichte

Gegengewichte in Beziehung Macht
Momentan wirtschaftlich und militärisch
In der Zukunft vielleicht nur geistig
(kurze eingeworfene Illusion)

Nichts bleibt stehen
Alles verändert sich

Anti-Terror-Krieg

Krieg gegen den internationalen Terrorismus
Krieg gegen Furcht und Schrecken
Krieg gegen Krieg

Mit Engelszungen kann man dem kaum begegnen,
aber mit Waschpulver.

Das Pulver besteht aus Toleranz, Verständnis,
Bildung und Milde.

Dann wird der Kopf genommen
in die Essenz eingetaucht
und gewartet wie der Geist anspricht.

Bei zu wenig Sauberkeit
wird dieser Vorgang wiederholt,
um den Hass, Unmut und die Agression
ganz zu vertreiben.

Und so wird aus dem Anti-Terror-Krieg
ein Anti-Terror-Sieg.

Kladderadatsch

Was reden sie da
das ist doch Quatsch

Machen sie sich lustig
Ironie der Kritik

ENGLISH POEMS

Bedtime

I have to go to bed now
but life is much to short
there are millions of things to do
millions of worlds to explore.

Why I have to sleep
tell me, tell me
just let me go, just let me go
and be, see and have glee.

Night is day and day is night
bright is dark and dark is bright

Stars you are my inspiration
sun you are my illumination

Time time time
offer me a clime
to my soul and life
while I strife....

I'd like to unhinge you
be active and just do do do

Chapeau 2U Maya

You were the Georg Sand
of our time
where your color was the crime.

But you held the strength in your hand
and fought against this social disparity
with the inner feeling for humanity.

Your weapons were just words and your voice
to rise up to the essential-imperative self-choice.

You were an activist in the human right movement
and stood there as a bulwark of freedom
composed and calmed with an inner wisdom

It was a great worldwide accomplishment
demolishing all the old infrastructures
and creating lasting and integrity pictures

Your weapons were just words and your voice
to rise up to the essential-imperative self-choice.

With your "on the pulse of the morning"
you encouraged man to have a dream
and reflected the mainstream.

You are just an amazing great human being
full of love for people and gave them hope
and developed integrity on mankind's slope

Your weapons were just words and your voice
to rise up to the essential-imperative self-choice.

Thanks a lot for your brave actions

showing that there are exceptions
you altered the course
in our human universe
May all your seeds find a place
and create an upright race.

Spitzweg the poor poet

I am going to miss
to write poetry and imaginations

Nowadays we can't live on art
of those musical words
which takes the soul apart
and play human chords

And still we need to write
and embrace the moment-side
what might be wrong or right

LOL

Isn't life just funny
We walk and whatever appears
Is again Mr. Murphy

We already shake our head and say
Give me a break.

But hurrah we got a new role
Job, without a job, and all those advantages.

Well what to do?
Laughing about the next stone
Sisyphus for a time
A real exciting job

And still alive
Looking up, enjoying the beauty
Homer's stories

Listening for more

Sometimes

Sometimes we meet somebody
And have this awesome sensation
This special feeling of knowing each other forever

Sometimes we meet somebody
To realize what we do not like
This special feeling of knowing the difference

Sometimes we meet somebody
And realize this is the one
This special feeling of staying the rest of life together

Sometimes we meet somebody
And have the pleasure to support
This special feeling is a need we have to express.

Sometimes we meet somebody
And have a great time
This special feeling of understanding each other without words

Sometimes we meet somebody
And somebody meets us

Take a look

We look in the eyes of a friend
And see whom we love

We look in the eyes of an enemy
And see what we could become

We look in the eyes of a child
And see who we should be

We look in the eyes of an animal
And see what we have in ourselves

We look in the mirror
And see who we are

Paper crossing the street

Wanting to cross the street
with the air and without feet
The wind just blows me up
I fly as I am crumbled up

Whose view is right

Which eyes are contemplating in the right way
Is there a right way at all, or just a matter of perspective?

Year 2222

Nowadays we are a free universe
most diverse.
We as long-term thinking earth inhabitants
amazing human ants.
We are curious and developed a cosmic care,
which we all share.
Since we stopped to give money inexplicable value
our intelligence grew.

Once we defined ourselves through material goods
still mentally in the backwoods.

For Gods sake, in previous centuries came a turning point
Clarification of facts we joint.

We discovered the space within us and our stellar system
with a new enriching self-esteem.
We started to live in peace, put up with other ideas and visions
all-encompassing unity the mission.
Still connected to this planet earth with solid attentiveness
aware of the expansiveness.
We found new conceptions of life beyond mind and matter
like a new universal trendsetter.

3333 again a small step and 5555 as well
attached to an progressive brain-cell
a constructive pell-mell
ringing the cosmic bell

Short-term relationship

We had a great time
It just did not work out

Long-term relationship

We have a great time
and just work on it every day

How different we are

You are so correct in all what you do
And I am sometimes a little rascal
You are perfect in your doings
And I am sometimes just laissez faire like
You are so demanding to yourself and others
And I am sometimes willing to let go
You are full of integrity and obey the rules
And I sometimes get out of the tight spot
You are and I am
And we are
Catch the star
Increase diversity
Within humanity
What else can we create
Than love in our inner state.

Mountains

Formed by millions of decades
Their shapes are just awesome
Walking along and become
A reflection to our own shades

They teach us to look
toward ourselves and contemplate
what we have in our own state
and which path we took

Here I stand, grateful for this beauty
Awesome wow, and I am humble
And always and every time I stumble
What our souls might reach and see

Let's go for it and find new traces
Here it's the inner understanding
And a long term strengthening
Far away from the human places.

Thanks for your silent advices

Sunrise

Awakening to a new day
Some they pray
Others just say
welcome you fantastic ray

Touching my eyelid
Gentle and still solid

Introduction of energy
A perfect synergy

Embracing continuously life
Learn openly and strife
In existence we dive
Millions of new starts arrive

The sun is enlightening
And new adventures are knocking

Sunshine produces activity
Like the fuel creativity

Sun, sun sun, come
And let me become

How I do admire
The human desire
Thoughts might inspire
And inflame the fire

The fire of existence
Capturing the essence

Horses

Powerful you are
Full of strength
We are friends
For a long time already

You are our feets

Catharina the Great

Sometimes we have to kill
And pay the bill
For humanity and our future
Cultural life to ensure

And some of us are full of energy
They need to express
Themselves in body synergy
And release stress.

Good ideas survive
And sometimes change life
Of a whole nation
Giving a new destination

Well done and the future will tell
What we did wrong what we did well
To foresee things would be great
But we never know and just create

Yellow and white

He had no time to regret
He just went back
And instead to reflect
He loved comfort
And showed me his back

Well I love you so much
I can't even tell through words
So I went back to us
Walking in the world of pleasing

He never thought of a future
In which love might rule
No inner sense to adventure
A new life to go for
And just to reschedule

Well I love you so much
I can't even tell through words
So I went back to us
Walking in the world of pleasing

Destiny is weird and unknown
we go on and discover
considering what was shown
and realize the next steps
that it's the heart we cover

Well I love you so much
I can't even tell through words
So I went back to us
Walking in the world of pleasing

No accusing no accusing at all
just bulling down the wall

Imagine

Imagine a world without greed
A world where integrity succeed

Imagine a world without hate
A world where love is the master of fate

Imagine a world without starvation
A world everybody has got access to education

Imagine a world without vanity
A world full of humble humanity

Imagine a world without gluttony
A world of sustainable harmony

Imagine a world without wrath
A world with an honorable path

Imaging, just imagine what it could be
A world in this universe

Dare you tell me what to do

Never give me orders again
They will come to you as pain
Suggestions I might contemplate
And compare them to my own state

Never threaten me with words
That's something what hurts
Considerations you might express
And they might be my success

Never try to lead my way
To your gods you might pray
I have my own trace
To find the eternal space

And if you want to change
Change first yourself

Easy to succeed with an open mind

You
& I
get
a we
& see
what to be

I
& You
get
& give
we live
attentive

Blunder

I dropped a brick
and turn the swizzle stick
What a slapstick?!

I'd like to take a break
for my own sake
and eat a cheesecake.

Fun for the spectator
but not for the initiator
being a convertor.

Life isn't always a bowl of cherries.
nor of delightful blueberries
We choose the life's ferries.

Welcome Murphy
embracing and see
his rigid lunacy

Humor the only way
to have fun and play
welcoming the day

Keep it in your mind
we always find
the beauty of mankind

Faults we have to make
for our own sake
and challenges to take.

The more we contemplate
we are the master of our fate

and move into a new gate

Let's be like we are
and be our own superstar

Reach out to mainly prevent
and just be content

Smile

What a wonderful gesture of joy
inspiring to everybody around
expressing happiness profound
and take life not seriously

Whatever may come along
we have to be strong
and learn with glee
what's out there to see

Myself is the best to laugh about
I am just a little human being
who honors every feeling
we are all more or less the same.

So let's pay life it's compliments
and look for refinements
to provoke pure happiness
and long-term aliveness

Whatever may happen and occur
Candide take it as it appears
without any tears
being the captain of his soul.

Who cares about riches rank or pride
Mr Jekle or Dr. Hyde
we are all the same
in this cosmic game

Always look on the bright
side of life
and strife
with a smile on your face.

Let's go for beauty and pleasure
everything is just a treasure
even so most diverse.
Thanks to be in this universe

Comfort

Every day great for sure
depending with which eyes we see
even a quarrel might be
in the end a revealing pleasure

Just paying life it's excitement
with all those little challenges
and creating contentment
without the need of revenges

Enjoying family and friends
with a curious and gentle approach
reaching each others hands
being each others coach

Comfortable of what ever occurs
with a smile on our lips
embracing life's flavors
and wiggling ones hips.

Far away of monotony
even so it's stony
composing a symphony
and dancing in harmony

Caprice 24

All emotions of life I feel
Ups and downs

Longing to live in fulfillment
And still stumble

Millions of roads to go
And none is leading to the inner peace

An intrinsic need to move on
No time to stop and rest, just interact

Deep emotions to find
Express them profoundly in musical words

A connection to the universe
Humbly aware of the material eternity

Beyond ordinary understanding
A gift offered to humans to open and see

What kind of God are you?

You let your son be killed in the name of love
You destroy people with good intensions
You have fun to gamble with the soul of beings
You play with Jobs souls to long for suicide
You are cold inside yourself
You stopped seeing with the heart
We humans forgive you and will find our own wisdom
We humans are happy to welcome you to love.
Jesus tried to open your mind,
And most people are like you
Selfish, poor and innocent

Poison in the air

It is only forever
We long for money
It is only forever
We sell our soul
Nobody can be blamed
We are into it
Nobody can be blamed
We go for it
Nothing we can do
My spaceship knows where to go
Nothing we can do
I am going to leave and say goodbye
We take our protein pills
And go on
We take our veggie pills
And go ahead
The stars look very different today
Things they were disappeared
The sky looks very different today
No more ground control

I am American

I am American and scream out loud
I am proud

I am American and bring peace
Democracy to increase

I am American and feel integrity
To bring humanity

I am American and belief in freedom
An inner stardom

I am American and support exploration
to create a vision

I am American and believe in a good life
For everybody alive

I am who I am and humbly say "Yes"
To progress

And build up new traces and places
To see happiness in all our faces

ISIS and Anti-terror victory

Why do you destroy
Destroying yourself
Why do you kill
Killing yourself
Why do you fight
Fighting yourself

Who are you
Find your innocent soul

What do you need
Find love within you

Where do you go
Go the road of peace

When do you open your eyes
To see beauty

Nobody is perfect
No religion is the only right one
Nobody is right
No idea the exclusive one

We all will send you love and understanding
We all will embrace your beautiful souls
We all believe in you and peace
We all believe in a better world
Wake up and open your eyes

See with the heart

Wake up and open your mind
understand the GO(O)D

Wake up it was a nightmare
Wake up, wake up

Hate, greed and all those things will disappear
And we create a wonderful life for all of us.

600 years of history are missing

Friendship

Show me your friends and
I will tell you who you are.

Without words they understand
and know your inner star.

Whenever you need support
they do their very best
and never spare any effort
befriending to invest.

Critics and reflections
of what might be right or wrong
those are worthy compassions
providing service to be strong.

And time is irrelevant
the feelings never change
its always most pleasant
experiences to exchange.

It's an interpersonal bond
including affection and honesty.
Spirits they correspond
with empathy and modesty.

Red Cross

What a fantastic organization
the idea to establish neutral protection
helping people in need.

What is interesting in deed
that Dunant the initiator
and the foundation creator
was removed from the institution
because of his humanistic devotion.

What are the motives of a jurist
to act like an antagonist?

Might be a profile neurosis
one of those diagnosis,
you often find in creatures
with poor and shabby features.

Pity for those who need to bare
these humans without inner care.
Mercy for those who have no heart
that they may find their better part.

In honor to brave men

In what do I believe
it's nothing anybody might achieve
Christianity or Buddhism
merely pure altruism.

In all the souls of humanity
born by the open minded sanity
just the names are different
and vary in how to understand.

I will not cease
and walk in peace
to seed the million love letters
without those religious fetters.

I care for life
and always strife
to create what I call pleasure
impossible to measure.

Being responsible and full of delight
building up and being bright.

Brainforming

So nuts I am, so nuts to pray
for human nature night and day
What can be formed?
What can be normed?
Which brains should we take
for the intelligence to reawake.

Loyalty

Is it the Royce's in philosophy
the object of all idealism
or is it like a honorable trophy
of normative moralism.

Allegiance to integrity
a virtue of great importance
Perpetual reliability
with permanent persistence.

Geocaching

Its not only nation wide
a special treasure to hide.

Sometimes a worthless object
might be able to connect

Different cultures on this planet
easy tracked by internet.

A great game of hide and seek
at times just to get a sneak peek
or take it with you and tuck it away
on another place it could stay.

Real fun to be a treasure hunter
proud of your founded plunder.

That's the easy connection
of human nature and gratification.

And full of joy and glee
behind borders to see.

Bloomsbury Group

Virginia Woolf, John Maynard Keynes, E. M. Forster
just to name some of the members
you were to English people to foster
the intellectual time with ambitious embers

Writers, intellectuals, philosophers and artists,
you like to change the world into better
we are all like you humans, self-seekers and altruists
active and ambitious trend-setter

What coincidences

I dropped my head
and instead
to pick it up again
I discovered my brain

I went across a bridge
thought of being rich
and found a gemstone
having a colorful tone

I was late on time
to meet a friend to dine
and an awesome rainbow
performed a beautiful show

My car went down
while heading to town
I had to hike
and avoid a strike

Looking for a rest
I invited myself as a guest
and encountered new friends
same like me gourmands

Millions of coincidences
amazing dependences
The destiny and it's tools
the fate and how it rules.

FM-2030

How might the future look like
more intelligent and less destructive?

A change from money is the most important
to humanity is the most exclusive?

The eventual goal is the fundamental transformation
by developing new technologies
to improve the worldwide human condition
and enhance human capacities

Intellectual, physical, and psychological progress
by uplifting the biological circumstances
which is almost reality and already in process
and will have wide-ranging influences.

Benevolence is based on profound emotions
like the sense of love and beauty
it lies beyond all technological creations,
which leads to real humanity.

The friendship to an animal

They do not think of what they might achieve
they are just friends and offer us relieve
they just listen to our soul and heart
they feel, see and perceive inward

They are not intelligent in the common way
they do not understand every word we say
they are sometimes exhausting and stressful
they are as well extravagant and effortful

In the end they are our best friend
they always offer us their hand
and with their emotional afflatus
they always try to protect us.

Specimens

Some of them are really weird, they stop at nothing
to gain pelf and wealth?
it's an evidence of incapacity and insane growing
detesting the universal health.

What for, some might ask, those who think more global
maybe it's just a narrow mind
an inner feeling of inferiority exposed non-verbal
toward integrity just blind.

Some of them are really amazing, they create just beauty
to gain happiness for all
it's an evidence of capacity and long term activity
admiring humanity to install.

What for, some might ask, those who think with smaller sight
maybe it's just an open mindset
looking beyond the curtain of just a single lifetime highlight
always moving ahead.

As an alien out of space, intelligent and advanced much more
I shake my head in astonishment
and know that centuries may pass by and they will explore
life' main accomplishment

Charlie Hebdo

Freedom of the press
Colorful is our dress
We point out the present
Our missions in the hand

Pourquoi
Toi et moi

Comedy the best art
for the wake-up start
Provoking in deed
Understanding may succeed.

Pourquoi
Toi et moi

Our duty to show reality
with using our ability
to look behind
with an open mind

Pourquoi
Toi et moi

And with respect
we reflect
To be more aware
about what to care

Pourquoi
Toi et moi

It's our view every single day
we never kill through what we say
It's just a picture of our time

And where there is a crime

Pourquoi
Toi et moi

We are strong and withour fear
And drive with the humorous gear
We never will cease
May freedom increase

Nous disons quelque chose
avec plaisanterie et la véridique rose

The best movies

The nominees for the category drama
The Shawshank Redemption
followed by Marlon's Godfather
and the four tale of Pulp fiction
Another one we seriously have to list
is the German story of Schindler's list
for the next one's we have to fight
between Fight club and The Dark Knight
Now the nominees for the category comedy
The Bucket List as a fantastic remedy
and the bachelor party The Hangover
here The Intouchables might take over
and not to forget Some like it hot
An old film and cute plot.
Crazy, Stupid, Love another one
and Home Alone which is also fun.

Leonardo

Born in the Medici-ruled Republic of Florence
As a result of a romantic coincidence
Already in his first years of being
His mind and spirit were corresponding
He had this very special talent
Transforming visions through the hand

With fourteen he left to find his fortune
The moment was just opportune
And as he wasn't a time-waster
Andrea del Verrocchio became his master
And taught him all the skills he needed
In all his multiple-prowess succeeded

They both designed wonderful art
Both toward each other the counterpart
David, Raphael or the Baptist of Christ
The Romans amazed and surprised
Verrochio had the true eye
And Leonardo reached the sky

He was a most talented musician
And as well an inspired physician
In the early 80is he moved to another city
Milan developing his artistic complexity
And starting to invent new machines
Agricultural and military engines

The Last Supper was created
An old idea defeated
Magdalena beside her friend
The night before the end
Subtle, an awesome reflection
Of an all too human affection.

To hide things from others
Slipping the passionate pothers
He wrote most ideas backwards
To escape all those cowards
Inventions beyond his contemporaries
Every epoch he got idle adversaries

Codex Atlanticus or Codex Leicester
He was an open requester
Observations and theories on astronomy
Exploration of the human anatomy
In all field he sailed like Thomas cook
The world for him a secret-open book

An artist of outstanding physical beauty,
Creating and discovering his duty
He cultivated his genius so brilliantly
He was constructive flamboyantly
All problems he studied he solved with ease
Farsightedness and knowledge to increase.

Vi veri universum vivus vici

Index

Bayerische Ansichten 5
Entsnowden 6
Promiskuität 7
Abstellgleis 8
Dilettantismus 9
Kurvendiskussion 10
Foodgasm 11
Fappieren 12
Staffellauf 13
Mammon 14
Mia san mia 15
Miteinander 16
Sonne 17
Ein kleines Schloß 18
Ameise 19
Die Seele schreit 20
Krieg 21
Tradition 22
Schildkröte 23
Tierischer Panzer 24
Klanggeflüster 25
Die Hand 26
Könner 27
Zigaretten 27

Anmut	29
Bayerischer Humor	30
Reichtum ist das Wichtigste	31
Leichtigkeit	32
Der Teppichhändler	33
Das Gewicht der Zeit	33
Generationen	35
Verhaltensgestört	36
Hausse und Baisse	37
Gladiatoren und Genies	38
Du	39
Burnout	40
Wikileaks	41
Weltklimagipfel	42
Wachstumsbeschleunigungsgesetz	43
Multipolare Welt	44
Anti-Terror-Krieg	45
Kladderadatsch	45
Bedtime	48
Chapeau 2U Maya	50
Spitzweg the poor poet	51
LOL	52
Sometimes	53
Take a look	54
Year 2222	55

Short-term relationship	55
Long-term relationship	56
How different we are	56
Mountains	57
Sunrise	58
Horses	59
Catharina the Great	59
Yellow and white	59
Paper crossing the street	54
Whose view is right	54
Imagine	61
Dare you tell me what to do	62
Easy to succeed with an open mind	62
Blunder	64
Smile	65
Comfort	68
Caprice 24	69
What kind of God are you?	70
Poison in the air	71
I am American	72
ISIS and Anti-terror victory	73
Friendship	75
Red Cross	76
In honor to brave men	77
Brainforming	78

Loyalty	78
Geocaching	79
Bloomsbury Group	79
What coincidences	81
FM-2030	82
The friendship to an animal	83
Specimens	84
Charlie Hebdo	85
The best movies	86
Leonardo	87